# SKIDOO

# SKIDOO

*A journey through the ghost towns*
*of the American West*

*by*
*Alex Capus*

*Translated by John Brownjohn*

Armchair Traveller
at the bookHaus

Originally published as *Skidoo: Meine Reise durch die Geisterstädte des Wilden Westen* by Alex Capus in 2012
Copyright © Carl Hanser Verlag München, 2012, 2013

Translation copyright © John Brownjohn, 2013
The moral right of the author has been asserted

First published in Great Britain in 2013 by
The Armchair Traveller at the bookHaus
70 Cadogan Place
London SW1X 9AH
*www.thearmchairtraveller.com*

A CIP record for this book is available from the British Library

Print ISBN: 978-1-907973-95-6
Ebook ISBN: 978-1-907973-96-3

Typeset in Garamond by MacGuru Ltd
Printed and bound in China by 1010 Printing International Ltd

This book has been translated with the support of the
Swiss Arts Council Pro Helvetia.

swiss arts council
**pr⊙helvetia**

# Contents

# BODIE

Wherever I go in the world, I always tend to linger in small towns that have only a few thousand inhabitants and remind me of Olten, my home town in Switzerland. Recently I found myself in Bodie, a gold-mining ghost town east of the snowy peaks of the Sierra Nevada in north-east California. Ten feet of snow can cover the place in winter – it's 8,379 feet above sea level – and the ground freezes so hard that in 1877, when people still lived and died there, graves had to be excavated with dynamite.

*Olten, Switzerland*

Boom, boom, boom! Detonations rent the frigid air from dawn to dusk, for the miners died like flies from diphtheria and pneumonia and the ground

*The graveyard, Bodie*

*Chinese
opium den*

trembled and window panes vibrated in crumbling putty and the townsfolk counted the explosions, knowing that each betokened a death.

The grandest funerals of all were held by the Chinese who ran the laundries, restaurants and opium dens on King Street, China being an advanced civilization thousands of years old in which people have been dying for far longer than they have in youthful America. When someone passed away in Chinatown, the mourners scattered snippets of red paper along the route to the graveyard, which was a mile out of town, to protect the soul of the deceased from attack by the devil. This was because the Evil One had to pick up every last snippet before he could get to work on the deceased's soul, by which time it would long since

*Bodie's hearse*

have disappeared into heaven.

So that the soul should lack for nothing on its journey, it was a traditional Chinese practice to deposit all kinds of food on the grave. The wind wafted the scent of spring rolls, Canton rice and sweet-and-sour duck breast across the surrounding hills, where it aroused the interest not only of wolves and bears, but also of the Paiute Indians, whose supplies often ran short at the end of winter. It is on record that the Paiute swiftly acquired a profound ethnographic knowledge of Chinese burial rites, and because they, for their part, had mastered the art of sneaking up on things unobserved and in silence, the finest feasts in Paiute villages were always held after Chinese funerals.

*Paiute Indians*

# PANAMINT CITY

Anyone fortunate enough to leave Bodie on horseback, with head erect and heart still beating, instead of vertically and heaven-bound, came sooner or later to the next small town, and from there to another small town, and from there to yet another. Bodie was surrounded by small towns, which were in turn surrounded by small towns indis-

*Lonely prospectors in Death Valley*

tinguishable from each other. The Wild West differed little in that respect from the Black Forest, Tuscany or the Alps, except that American small towns are not situated within sight of each other, but separated by

tracts of land capable of swallowing up the whole of the Black Forest, all of Tuscany, and the entire Swiss Alps.

Within these expanses there are fire-spewing volcanoes and mountains of magnetic iron, petrified

*Grizzly bear*

9

forests, boiling hot rivers and frightful chasms that yawn so deep into the earth's interior you feel you're looking at the dawn of Creation and wouldn't be surprised to see dinosaurs browsing down there. The trees soar into the sky, so tall and massive you can bore holes through the trunks and drive carriages through them, and the bears, when they rise on their hind paws to attack, are not the height of a man but twice or three times as tall. I can well imagine how terrified the earliest prospectors of 1849 must have been – men who until a few months previously had been bank clerks

*Snowy mountains overlooking Death Valley*

*Heavy transport in Death Valley*

in Cracow or policemen in Toulouse or farmhands in Tuscany – the first time they saw a grizzly bounding towards them, and how horrified they would have been by the fact that the beast did not drop dead when you emptied the magazine of your Smith & Wesson into its fur, and I wonder why, given that America's flora, fauna, topography and climate were so far off the human scale, those people didn't simply turn around and go home to Cracow, Toulouse or Tuscany.

Many of them really did turn around. There are also said to have been some who kept on heading west until they had rounded the globe and ended up back in Europe. But a remarkable number – possibly because they lacked the price of a passage home – put down roots on the way, usually in small towns, because nearly all American towns were small. In 1875, for instance, the Californian coastal settlement of Los Angeles had 7,000 inhabitants, only twice as many as 19th-century Olten, my home town.

On the western edge of Death Valley lies Panamint City, which is reputed to have been founded by some

*An unfortunate man at journey's end*

11

*Wells Fargo wagon*

desperados who had attacked a Wells Fargo stagecoach and fled with their haul to the remote Surprise Canyon to wait until the guardians of the law either lost their urge to pursue them or transferred it to the next stagecoach robbers. That could take a very long time or a very short one. On the one hand, Wells Fargo had made it a rule to put 300 dollars on the head of every robber, regardless of identity; on the other, stagecoaches were always being robbed, and bounty hunters tended to hunt the most recent quarry because any traces of earlier robberies quickly disappeared in the trackless West.

The bandits waited for three days, two weeks, a month. They had brought plenty of food with them and got their drinking water from a small stream at the foot of the canyon. The canyon was situated in the Shoshone Indians' tribal area, but there was no sign of the Indians themselves. Although a little vegetation grew on the banks of the stream, the rest of the terrain was all stones and rattlesnakes. From time to time a rabbit or a coyote would scamper past. By day the desperados played cards; at night they roasted a rabbit or a coyote.

In movies a bandit's daily routine looks picturesque and romantic, but the reality of life outside the law was insufferably monotonous and boring. Personally, I only once renounced the company of women and children – this was in the late summer of 1964 – in order to lead an outlaw's life of freedom and independence behind the bramble hedge. I had to cut this venture short after only a few hours because I realized that the company of earthworms, snails and ants would not entirely satisfy me in the long term.

*The author in late summer 1964, somewhere in Normandy*

At some stage, one of the desperados filled in time by going for a walk up the side of the canyon. He hummed a tune and picked some wild thyme with which to season the next roast rabbit, then sat down in the shade of an overhanging rock and tossed stones at lizards standing stock-still in the blazing sun as they diagonally raised one foreleg and one hind leg in the air to cool them. The bandit suddenly noticed a strangely glittering quality about the stone he was about to

*Thermal dance of a lizard cooling its hot feet*

throw. Having hammered it to bits with his pistol butt, he discovered that it contained a large proportion of high-grade silver. He summoned his friends, and it transpired that Surprise Canyon embraced an area five miles long and two-and-a-half wide in which veins of silver ran close together.

The men were overjoyed by their discovery. They were now richer than they could ever have become by robbing stagecoaches. The only trouble was, their wealth would have to remain hypothetical for as long as the Wells Fargo stagecoach incident prevented their return to legality. The record would have to be wiped clean in some way.

At that time in Virginia City, Nevada, there was a state senator named William W. Stewart who had made a fortune as a lawyer specializing in prospectors' licences and was known to be helpful in such cases. Legend has it that the robbers decided to fill their saddlebags with silver ore, ride to Virginia City, and ask this man for help. The senator thereupon asked Wells Fargo how many kilograms or hundredweight of silver it would take to cancel out the regrettable stagecoach business. One gathers that Wells Fargo promptly quoted a weight – Senator Stewart spoke many years later of 12,000 to 20,000 dollars – and the criminal aspect of the matter was tacitly waived.

Once this had been settled, Senator Stewart bought the bandits' claims in Surprise Canyon and, in January 1874, founded not just one mining company but nine of them, so as to enable as many investors as possible to participate

*Senator William W. Stewart*

in the expected silver boom. He offered the shares on the San Francisco stock market for a total price of 50 million dollars.

In the ensuing months, Panamint City sprouted from the desert floor of Surprise Canyon under the eyes of the Shoshone Indians. In March the place boasted 125 inhabitants; by the year's end there were 2,000. In September alone, 150 itinerant Chinese labourers arrived. As in nearly all small towns in the Wild West, the proportion of male inhabitants to female exceeded 90 per cent, and by far the biggest age group was that of 18 to 25-year-olds.

Upwards of a dozen saloons opened on either side of the main street. While many were just huts or tents, others embellished themselves with crystal chandeliers and cut-glass mirrors and lined their walls with gold silk. The brothel-keeper Martha Camp and her girls set up shop in Little Chief Canyon, a little way off the main street. There being no hospital in Panamint City, they also offered their services – for a fee – as nurses. They splinted broken legs and treated gunshot wounds, and if a miner went down with fever they brought him oatmeal porridge and plied him with tea.

Within a few weeks the town had acquired two banks, a cobbler and a barber, three physicians, four lawyers, a pharmacist, a butcher, and a jeweller. On 26 November 1874 the first issue of the *Panamint News* appeared, its chief function being to spread favourable reports designed to boost share prices. There never was a school or a church in Panamint City, nor a sheriff, court-house or jail. In the five months from November 1874 to March 1875, five people were shot dead in the little town, but no one was ever convicted of those crimes. The young and universally popular attorney William Cassius Smith, who acted as a provisional magistrate, ruled that self-defence had been involved in every case.

It was a particularly happy day when a German brewer named Louis Munzinger arrived in Panamint City with a covered wagon full of brewing equipment, his aim being to quench the gold miners' thirst with German beer. He was 41 years old and had lived in America for seven years, and seated on the box beside him was his very, very young wife Ada. At 15, she was already carrying her second infant in her arms and had been travelling the Wild West at her husband's side for at least three years.

I'd like to know more about that girl. I'd like to know what had prompted an 11 or 12-year-old to entrust her fate to a man three times her age. I'd like to know if her father and mother had succumbed to starvation, or to some disease or crime, or if she had run away from her parental home because life elsewhere could not be worse. I'd like to know if her choice of Louis Munzinger as her protector – he is reported to have been a good-natured bear of a man – was dictated by shrewd calculation, and if she knew, even at so young

*Sonora*

*Josef Munzinger*

an age, what a woman had to do to keep a man at her side.

I know none of these things. I don't know them because newspapers seldom mentioned women. They committed fewer criminal offences, and when they married they shed their maiden names and disappeared from their family tree, and if they came into money and bought a house, the law prescribed that they must have a husband to sign the contracts for them. That is why all I know for certain is that Ada's maiden name was Galarone, which smacks of Italian roots, that she was born at Sonora, the Californian gold-mining town, in 1859, and that she must have crossed Louis Munzinger's path no later than 1871.

So the brewer was called Munzinger. The discovery of his family name caused me some temporary excitement, because Munzingers are strongly represented in my native Olten, both quantitatively and qualitatively. Many of the Olten Munzingers are called Hans or Johann; in fact the Hans/Johann line can be traced back over four centuries. An Oltner named Josef Munzinger became the young Swiss Federation's finance minister in 1848 and is regarded as the father of the Swiss franc, his son Walter drafted the Swiss law of contracts, and the latter's brother, Werner, was an African explorer. The family has also produced several distinguished musicians, a female traveller to China named Mizzi, and several painters. I myself have a pretty little oil painting by a Hans Munzinger hanging in my kitchen, and every few months I get my hair cut by my friend Pit or his sister Katrin, both of whom are Oltner Munzingers of the 18th generation. I would thus have been delighted to augment their ancestral portrait gallery with a brewer from Death Valley. In the censuses of 1870, 1880 and 1890, however, Louis Munzinger gave his birthplace as Bavaria, not Olten. I was loath to accept this at face value, because had I been a brewer in America I might also have disavowed my native town and posed as a Bavarian for PR purposes. So I descended his family tree, branch by branch, and eventually came to the conclusion that Louis must also have been an

*Pit Munzinger*

*The old sawmill at Olten on the Aare, painted by Hans Munzinger in 1929*

Oltner. I'm fairly sure of this. It's very probable – or at least, not out of the question.

However, I'm bound to concede that Louis was Bavarian by birth, having first seen the light on 9 November 1832 at Bruchmühlbach in Rheinpfalz, halfway between Saarbrücken and Mannheim. Although this town is situated on the French border, far to the west of Bavaria by today's reckoning, the Congress of Vienna had awarded the district to the Kingdom of Bavaria after the Napoleonic Wars.

Climbing Louis Munzinger's family tree, one comes across his father, Johann (!) Christian, also born in Bruchmühlbach in 1798, and his grandfather Johann (!) Adam (b. 1765), who was Imperial Postmaster at Bruchmühlbach and had put Emperor Napoleon up for the night on his retreat from Moscow. Another branch higher we find Great-Grandfather Johann Adam (b. 1721), likewise postmaster of Bruchmühlbach, Great-Great-Grandfather Johann Philipp (b. 1689), founder of the post office in Bruchmühlbach, and finally Great-Great-Great-Grandfather Hans

Wilhelm (b. circa 1660), a farmer.

But local records attest that the latter's father, Great-Great-Great-Great-Grandfather Hans Reinhard Munzinger (b. circa 1630), was not a native Bruch-

*Bruchmühlbach*

mühlbacher – I knew it! – but an immigrant from Switzerland. That he hailed from Olten cannot be proved beyond all doubt because he does not appear in the Olten Munzingers' family tree. However, since an estimated 90 per cent of Swiss Munzingers lived in Olten at the time and there was, as far as is known, no Hans Reinhard Munzinger in the rest of Switzerland, I venture to assert that he came from Olten.

It is possible that he emigrated to the Pfalz before the age of 20 and was thus excluded from the family tree. Or he may have been conscripted into the French army, as was then customary. Or his branch of the family had settled in one of the farming

*Napoleon Bonaparte*

21

villages outside town whose inhabitants were never listed in writing.

At all events, Hans Reinhard Munzinger the Swiss moved to the Pfalz, which had been depopulated by the Thirty Years' War, in 1661. On 7 May of that year he purchased a garden plot in Bruchmühlbach, which means that his great-great-great-great-grandson Louis Munzinger, the Death Valley brewer, although not a son of my native town, was its great-great-great-great-nephew in the sixth degree. Or may have been.

Climbing back up the Pfalz Munzingers' family tree, one finds that the Swiss immigrant had, in addition to the aforesaid Hans Wilhelm (b. 1660), an older son

*Adolf Hitler*

named Hans Theobald (b. 1657), whose son Hans Michel (b. 1679) became a farmer in the neighbouring village of Gerhardsbrunn and left the farm to his son and namesake, Hans Michel (b. 1708). The latter left it to his son Johann Adam (b. 1745), who handed it over to his son Johann Jakob (b. 1768). Then came Jakob (b. 1807), who became by marriage a publican, brewer, and mayor of neighbouring Quirnbach, and was one of the ringleaders of the Pfalz Revolution of 1849. His son Adolf (b. 1834) took over his father's brewery and mayoralty but was unable to bequeath them both to his first-born son Ernst August (b. 1855) because the latter emigrated to Russia to brew beer with his brothers Adolf and Freidrich.

The last male scion of this branch of the Munzinger family was Ernst Gustav Munzinger (1887–1945). He went down in history because, having initially been an enthusiastic Nazi, he joined the circle of conspirators involved in the attempt on Hitler's life on 20 July 1944. On the night of 23 April 1945, he and 14 other resistance fighters were shot by the Gestapo in Invalidenstrasse, Berlin. In the few extant photographs of him he could be the brother of my Olten friend Pit Munzinger. To my mind, this is sufficient proof that we Oltners were responsible not only for brewing beer in Death Valley, but for an attempt on Hitler's life. Even if everything didn't always go according to plan.

*Ernst Gustav Munzinger*

But let us go back beyond the Sierra Nevada, where Louis Munzinger turned up in 1870, impregnated and married a

23

*Shoshone tepee village*

young girl named Ada Galar-one, and brewed beer in the trading post of Lone Pine until, at half past two on the night of 26 March 1872, the place was shaken by a powerful earthquake felt from Canada in the north to Panama in the south. The Shoshone Indians in the surrounding tepee villages were only briefly woken by it and slept on, but the brick buildings in the Lone Pine were reduced to rubble within seconds. Thirty of the 300 inhabitants died, and 52 of 59 buildings collapsed.

Louis and Ada Munzinger were unscathed, but their first-born son, Louis Munzinger Jr., was crushed to death by some falling masonry. They buried him next morning in the dusty soil, which continued to be shaken for a week by over 1,000 aftershocks. Modern geologists estimate that the first shock measured 7.5 to 8 on the Richter scale, and that in the Lone Pine rift valley an earthquake of such magnitude occurs only every three to four thousand years.

On 4 July of the following year, when she was only just 14, Ada Munzinger gave birth to a second baby boy who was also christened Louis Jr. and, because of his date of birth, given the patriotic middle name 'Washington'. A few months later, when the Panamint City boom began, Louis Munzinger

*Louis Munzinger's brewery*

loaded his brewing utensils into a covered wagon and headed for Surprise Canyon with his wife and infant son. He dug a hole in the hillside, found some sufficiently soft water, and started brewing beer. His best customer was the 'Inyo Saloon', which was popular with the miners because of the big billiard table the landlord had ordered from San Francisco, whence it had been hauled 500 miles by a team of oxen.

The ore extracted in Surprise Canyon contained silver worth a respectable 900 dollars a ton. Share prices rose and Senator Stewart became temporarily wealthy. However, Panamint City was a lawless place where no day went by without a shooting. Lurking in the surrounding hillsides were all manner of shady characters eager to secure a share in the town's newfound prosperity. The four bandits who had triggered

*The big ore-crushing mill, Panamint City*

the silver boom were also still in the area, living it up, without any discernible form of livelihood, on the money they had quite legally acquired from Senator Stewart.

One problem affecting the mining company derived from the fact that Wells Fargo refused, on security grounds, to haul the silver to the strongrooms of the big banks in San Francisco. Senator Stewart solved this problem by casting it in ingots weighing as much as 400 pounds, not in handy bars. This rendered them so theft-proof that they could be trundled past the crooks and bandits and out of Surprise Canyon in ordinary, unguarded wagons.

Even during the second year of operation, however, it became apparent that the silver deposits were only shallow. No sooner had the miners driven shafts a few yards into the mountainside than the silver content dramatically decreased. It was clear that the veins would soon be exhausted. What was more, world demand for silver slumped because Germany, having received five billion gold francs in reparation payments from France after winning the Franco-German War, had stopped minting silver thalers. The result was a chain reaction in which all the industrial nations switched from silver to the gold standard. Shares in the Panamint companies, already hit by the collapse of the Viennese stock market, went into free fall. Senator Stewart sustained big losses, although some critics claimed that he had knowingly staged a short-lived boom from the outset, his aim being to extract money from the pockets of gullible investors with criminal intent.

In the middle of May the mining company suspended operations. One saloon after another closed down, the itinerant Chinese labourers moved 200 miles north to the gold-mining town of Bodie, which was just experiencing its initial boom, and Martha Camp and her girls left Little Chief Canyon. The stagecoach no longer came daily but only once a month. On 21 October 1875 the *Panamint News* ceased publication. The final catastrophe occurred on 24 July 1876, when a cloudburst descended on the mountains. The stream the stagecoach

*Panamint City today*

27

bandits had camped beside three years earlier became a raging torrent. The remaining inhabitants of Panamint City, Louis Munzinger and his wife and child among them, managed to scramble to safety up the mountainside, but nearly all the houses and saloons were swept away, likewise the post office, the banks, the law office, the cobbler's workshop and the brewery.

The billiard table from the 'Inyo Saloon' was so heavy it managed to withstand the force of the deluge. When the flood subsided and the clouds dispersed, there it remained, standing in the open air, its green baize bleaching in the desert sun.

The mining companies had no money to spend on reconstruction and declared themselves bankrupt. Louis Munzinger retrieved his brewing equipment from the ruins and set off to find a new home in his covered wagon. At some point his child-wife Ada ran off, without Louis Washington Jr. but, one hopes, accompanied by some hot-blooded youth of her own age. When last heard of in 1897, she was somewhere down south, running a post-house on the old desert road between Lone Pine and Los Angeles.

Louis Munzinger settled down five days' journey north of Panamint City in Bishop, Inyo County,

*Tombstone of Louis Munzinger Sr.*

*Tombstone of Louis Munzinger Jr.*

where he continued to brew beer and became a prosperous saloon-keeper. Louis Washington Jr. remained – and brewed beer – with his father until the old man died. In 1899 he married a woman named Leonora May Deck and had two daughters whom he christened Leonora and Estelle and brought up in his father's home, which, according to the girls, was a happy household. When Louis Sr. became bedridden, his son devotedly nursed him until his death on 6 January 1913. Sixteen years later, when Louis Washington also died on the morning of 22 January 1929, he was buried beside his father in the East Line Street Cemetery (Sector 32, Row 9, Graves 14 and 15).

Only a few steadfast souls continued to live in the ruins of Panamint City in the following years, digging for silver on their own account and playing billards on the open-air table from the 'Inyo Saloon' until the baize perished, the cues warped, and the ivory balls were worn away to ovoids.

And, when everything was finally over, the Shoshone Indians who had lived in Surprise Canyon for millennia returned. They had always known it was unwise to settle on the valley floor because it was inundated every few years.

# SKIDOO

Twenty-five miles north of Surprise Canyon, high up in the Panamint range, is a ghost town named Skidoo. In the spring of 1908 there were several gold mines there, as well as a post and telegraph office and the General Trading

*Typical saloon tent in Death Valley*

Store, which doubled as the local branch of the Southern California Bank. On the other side of the street was the Gold Seal Saloon, a timber and canvas establishment in which hard men consorted with a handful of ladies who claimed to be French.

The co-owner of the Gold Seal Saloon was a man named Joseph Simpson, known as Hootch because of his unrivalled ability to put away cheap liquor. His binges did not last just one evening or night, but could go on for three or four and sometimes five days in succession. When Hootch was drunk he became mean, roistering around town and brandishing his gun. He had moved from Reno, where he had worked as a part-time pimp and bartender and become a local celebrity. In Independence in the summer of 1907 he had been

Hotel

sentenced to a term of imprisonment, suspended, for shooting up the chandelier in a hotel lobby.

His final binge ended late one Sunday morning, 19 April 1908, in his own saloon. He had been drinking alone since dawn because everyone else had gone to bed. At 11.00 Hootch ran out of liquor and had no money either, having probably spent it on the French women. If he wanted to go on drinking he needed to get hold of some cash.

So he got to his feet and went outside. The weather was fine, the *Skidoo News* reported later, and the midday sun was blazing down out of a cloudless sky. The street was deserted save for a few dogs slinking along in the shade in the lee of the buildings. Hootch's eyes were bloodshot. Gun in hand, he staggered over to the General Trading Store and planted himself in front of the counter.

'Hey, Jim,' he said to his friend Jim Arnold, who combined the functions of storekeeper, gold miner and branch manager of the Southern California Bank, 'gimme twenty dollars.'

In retrospect one must assume that Hootch did not have any skullduggery in mind; he simply needed 20 dollars, that was all. As Jim Arnold saw it, however, Hootch was standing at the counter of the Southern California Bank, demanding money with a loaded gun in his hand. Fond though he was of his friend Hootch, Jim could not sanction a bank robbery, so he chucked him out, advising him to cool it and put his head down for a few hours.

Hootch did so. He went back to the Gold Seal Saloon and put his head down. When he awoke three hours later, however, he had a headache and was thirsty. And because he still had no liquor and no money, he returned to the General Trading Store and once more levelled his gun at Jim Arnold's chest. Witnesses testified that the following dialogue then took place:

'What have you got against me, Jim?'

*Mine shaft entrance, Skidoo*

'Oh Hootch, I've nothing against you.'

'Yes, you have. Get ready to die. I'm going to shoot you.'

So saying, Hootch Simpson shot his friend Jim Arnold in the chest.

The shot loudly punctured the little town's Sunday afternoon stupor and mine workers came running from all directions, most of them inadequately attired and almost all carrying some kind of firearm. Deputy Sheriff Henry Sellers handcuffed the still obstreperous Hootch and, because Skidoo had no jail, locked him up in an empty shed. Some men carried gravely wounded Jim Arnold over to the house of Dr Reginald MacDonald, the township's only physician, where he died early that evening.

The deputy sheriff launched an immediate inquiry. All the eye-witnesses agreed that Hootch Simpson had, shortly after eleven that morning, presented himself at the counter of the Southern California Bank, pointed a loaded pistol, and demanded twenty dollars. This, they stated, definitely amounted to an attempted bank robbery; the paltriness of the sum involved did not affect its criminality. As to the second, far more serious offence, eye-witnesses were also unanimous that three hours later, or shortly after two in the afternoon, Hootch had once more barged into the General Trading Store and, after a brief conversation with Jim Arnold, deliberately shot him in the chest.

This had been wanton, cold-blooded murder, every inhabitant of Skidoo was clear on that score. Hootch Simpson would end on the gallows in accordance with the written and unwritten laws of the West, but the road there was a long one. First, the deputy sheriff would be duty-bound to write a report of the case and wire it to the sheriff in Independence, 100 miles away. The latter would then ride over to Skidoo – a three-day trip – and conduct an inquiry of his own. After that, Hootch would be conveyed to the district jail in Independence. This would herald the start of lengthy criminal proceedings that would cost taxpayers many thousands of dollars and could have only one correct outcome – though whether it would ever come to that was very uncertain.

Fatal shootings were an everyday occurrence in the little towns of Inyo County, so the judicial authorities were chronically overloaded with work. Hootch

Simpson's murderous act would be ancient history within a few months, and if he pleaded self-defence he would probably be released for lack of evidence and simply warned never to show his face in the district again.

On Monday morning, when the workers went back to the silver mines, Hootch Simpson awoke from his delirium in a semi-sober condition. Although still handcuffed, he behaved in an incomprehensibly cheerful manner, calling himelf 'a genuine hero' and 'a Bohemian'.

On Tuesday clouds rolled in. Bank manager Jim Arnold was laid to rest in the graveyard in a simple ceremony.

On Wednesday the clouds dispersed and the sweltering heat returned. The little town was unusually quiet. The mine workers knocked off punctually and went home, the saloons remained empty. One hour after nightfall every lighted window went dark. People seemed to have gone to bed early. At midnight, however, several dozen men assembled in the gloomy main street and made their way to the shed that served as Hootch's jail. Without speaking, they pushed past Deputy Sheriff Sellers, broke the door down, and dragged Hootch Simpson out. Sellers later asserted that the men were armed and had outnumbered him fifty to one, and no, he couldn't identify any of them because of the handkerchiefs over their faces.

When the next day dawned, Hootch Simpson's highly visible corpse was hanging from a telephone pole in the main street with a noose around its neck. The deputy sheriff cut him down, then had him carried into the Gold Seal Saloon, where Dr MacDonald pronounced Joseph Simpson dead and took two photographs, one of which showed him lying on a table. In order to render the second photograph more memorable, MacDonald had the dead man handcuffed and hanged once more with a rope around his neck. For reasons of discretion, however, he was suspended from one of the beams inside the saloon tent, not outside from the telephone pole.

When questioned, all the inhabitants of Skidoo claimed that they were fast asleep and had heard and seen nothing out of the ordinary because it was an unusually dark and silent night. A glance at the lunar calendar for 1908 does, in fact, confirm that the relevant night in California was moonless. In his report, the sheriff came to the conclusion that Hootch Simpson

*Joe 'Hootch' Simpson hanged for the second time*

had 'died of strangulation at the hands of unknown parties', and he released his body for burial.

The problem was that the only spare plot in the little cemetery was next to that of Jim Arnold, and the townsfolk of Skidoo considered it unbefitting to unite the murderer in death with his victim. Eventually, some compassionate soul fetched the corpse from the saloon, stowed it in a wooden box, hefted this on to a handcart, and wheeled it out of town to an abandoned gold miner's shaft, where Hootch was laid to rest.

The following day, Skidoo was bombarded with headlines. 'Butcher lynched by furious miners,' splashed the *Los Angeles Herald*. 'Citizens of Skidoo take the law into their own hands. Sheriff overpowered.'

'Murderer lynched with general approval', wrote MR MacLeod, editor of the *Skidoo News*. 'That such a man should be at large,' he commented at the conclusion of a full-page article, 'is not only a national shame, but a national crime. The method of disposing of such in the way that happened here is JUST, CHEAP and SALUTARY in the lesson it conveys. Local gunmen are already in a chastened frame of mind. Would-be bad men, as they bowl along the road on their triumphal entry of Skidoo, will note the number, the stoutness, the great convenience of the telephone poles, and reflect thereon.'

Then life resumed its course and Skidoo went the way of all ghost towns. The veins of gold in the mountain ran out. A month after Hootch's death the water line that supplied the gold mine with energy by way of a waterwheel burst. The company could not afford to replace it because its shares had halved in value during the banking crisis of 1907. Hundreds of labourers moved out. The *Skidoo News* ceased publication and its printing press was sold off to neighbouring Keeler.

The curtain had fallen, the affair was over. Newspapers turned their attention to other sensations. They reported on oil strikes in Iran and the summer Olympic Games in London. New gold deposits were discovered, new companies formed, new murders committed.

But six weeks after the drama the *New York Times* of 3 June 1908 carried a small advertisement:

# SEEK LYNCHED MAN'S WIDOW.

## Skidoo Citizens Will See That Mrs. Joseph Simpson Gets $25,000.

RENO, Nev., June 2.—Friends of Joseph Simpson, who was lynched at Skidoo for shooting a saloon man, are trying to find his widow. It is stated that he left more than $25,000 and that his wife will receive it if she will apply for it.

How the *New York Times* came to describe Jim Arnold, a bank employee, as a 'saloon man' is not known and was probably due to slipshod research on the part of the journalist in question. The information that Hootch Simpson possessed $25,000 is important because it means that he was far from being a poor wretch compelled to become a bank robber when he came to the end of a long binge with no more small change in his pocket. On the contrary, Hootch was a well-to-do man who could simply go to the bank whenever he needed money.

It has become apparent, a century after the event, that an injustice was done to Joseph Simpson on 19 April 1908. He was mortally offended when Jim Arnold refused him 20 dollars and threw him out into the street – he, who had $25,000 deposited with the South California Bank. He may have brandished a pistol that morning, but it would never for a moment have occurred to him to raid his own bank. He had simply needed 20 dollars in order to go on boozing for another 24 hours. The citizens of Skidoo must have become painfully aware of this when they found the bank book among his personal effects.

I don't know if his widow ever came into the money. The *New York Times* never mentioned Hootch Simpson's name again or printed any more reports from Skidoo.

However, it was a while before his maltreated body really found eternal rest. The very night after its unceremonious disposal, Dr MacDonald armed himself with a scalpel and crept out of town to the abandoned mine shaft, where he cut off Hootch Simpson's head and took it home to examine it for

*Dr Reginald MacDonald (right) with an unknown patient*

syphilitic lesions and other abnormalities. Having satisfied his curiosity, he left the gory object on an anthill until most of the flesh had gone, then boiled the skull for three days and henceforth kept it in a linen bag beneath the floorboards, where one of his successors chanced to find it years later. Thereafter, Hootch's skull was passed from hand to hand. In the middle of the 20th century it was offered as an exhibit to a local museum, which could not accept it, because although the museum statutes permitted the acceptance of Native American bones, those of white men were barred on religious grounds.

What happened to the rest of Hootch Simpson's remains is obscure. Many people say that his headless skeleton came to light again years later, when an unsuspecting gold miner was working in the shaft. Others claim that a few days after his death, some ladies of dubious reputation drove over from Beatty in a covered wagon, their intention being to give Hootch's twice-hanged, once-decapitated body a Christian burial. However, the stench became so intolerable on their return trip through the diabolical heat of Death Valley that the ladies abandoned their plan and dumped Hootch somewhere by the roadside.

# SALT WELLS

You can tell spring is coming to the heart of Death Valley by the way the lizards there lie on their backs to cool their hot feet, and when they start blowing on them summer isn't far off. Leave a hen's egg in the sun early in the morning and you can peel it, hard-boiled, at midday. The dead don't crumble away to dust; they become desiccated mummies within a few hours.

In 1874 a man named Jonathan Newhouse made headlines in this area by claiming to have invented a protective suit against heatstroke and sunstroke. According to the *Territorial Enterprise* of Virginia City, this consisted of a long, close-fitting jacket sewn together out of inch-thick sponge and a cap of the same material. Beneath his right arm Jonathan Newhouse carried a rubber pouch from which a tube connected to the top of his cap ensured that the solar armour was permanently saturated with water, the evaporation of which produced considerable superficial cooling. To keep his outfit moist, all the desert trekker had to do was squeeze the pouch occasionally with his right arm.

*Editorial office of the* Territorial Enterprise

47

Newspaper reports stated that Jonathan Newhouse was 47 years old and had come from Ohio to try out his invention under the most rigorous conditions imaginable. According to the *Territorial Enterprise*, he left the last human habitation on 27 June, stating that he would be back within two days. It was not, however, Newhouse who appeared on 29 June, but an Indian who could speak little English and excitedly gestured to his listeners to follow him. After riding 20 miles into the heart of the desert, the Indian pointed out a human figure leaning against a rock in the murderous heat. It was Newhouse, frozen stiff inside his solar armour. His beard was filmed with frost, and despite the heat of the midday sun, which must have exceeded 150 degrees Fahrenheit in summer, there was an icicle dangling from his nose. The *Territorial Enterprise* concluded by saying that Newhouse had 'perished miserably' in the middle of Death Valley because his invention had worked too well and he had been unable to release himself from his frozen armour.

The story was taken up by many newspapers. On 7 July it was published verbatim by the *San Francisco Examiner*, on 10 July by the *New York Times*, and on 25 July by the *Scientific American*. It then crossed the Atlantic and

## SAD FATE OF A NEVADA INVENTOR.

### From the Virginia City Enterprise.

A gentleman who has just arrived from the borax fields of the desert regions surrounding the town of Columbus, in the eastern part of this State, gives us the following account of the sad fate of Mr. Jonathan Newhouse, a man of considerable inventive genius. Mr. Newhouse had constructed what he called a "solar armor," an apparatus intended to protect the wearer from the fierce heat of the sun in crossing deserts and burning alkali plains. The armor consisted of a long, close-fitting jacket made of common sponge, and a cap or hood of the same material; both jacket and hood being about an inch in thickness. Before starting across a desert this armor was to be saturated with water. Under the right arm was suspended an India-rubber sack filled with water and having a small gutta-percha tube leading to the top of the hood. In order to keep the armor moist, all that was necessary to be done by the traveler, as he progressed over the burning sands, was to press the sack occasionally, when a small quantity of water would be forced up and thoroughly saturate the hood and the jacket below it. Thus, by the evaporation of the moisture in the armor, it was calculated might be produced almost any degree of cold. Mr. Newhouse went down to Death Valley, determined to try the experiment of crossing that terrible place in his armor. He started out into the valley one morning from the camp nearest its borders, telling the men at the camp, as they laced his armor on his back, that he would return in two days. The next day an Indian, who could speak but a few words of English, came to the camp in a great state of excitement. He made the men understand that he wanted them to follow him. At the distance of about twenty miles out into the desert the Indian pointed to a human figure seated against a rock. Approaching they found it to be Newhouse, still in his armor. He was dead and frozen stiff. His beard was covered with frost, and—though the noonday sun poured down its fiercest rays—an icicle over a foot in length hung from his nose. There he had perished miserably, because his armor had worked but too well, and because it was laced up behind where he could not reach the fastenings.

did the rounds of Great Britain. The London *Times*, the *York Herald* and the *Bath Chronicle* printed it under the heading 'Too Successful', likewise the *Sheffield Daily Telegraph* and the *Edinburgh Evening News*.

Only London's *Daily Telegraph*, one of the most important newspapers in the British Empire and, thus, in the world, expressed faint doubts as to whether it was possible to generate such low temperatures by means of evaporation alone. 'The marvellous stories which come from "the plains" are apt to be received with incredulity by our transatlantic kinsmen who dwell upon the Eastern seaboard of the United States. We confess that, although the fate of Mr Newhouse is related by the Western journal *au grand sérieux*, we should require some additional information before we unhesitatingly accept it. But everyone who has iced a bottle of wine by wrapping a wet cloth round it and putting it in a draught must have noticed how great is the cold that evaporation of moisture produces. For these reasons we are disposed to accept the tale from Virginia City in the same frame of mind which Herodotus, the Father of History,

*William Wright, alias Dan de Quille*

usually assumed when he repeated some marvel that had reached him – that is to say, we are neither prepared to disbelieve it wholly nor to credit it without question.'

The next day, a copy of the *Daily Telegraph* left for New York with the American mail aboard a steamship, crossed the broad plains of the Middle West by train and stagecoach, and three weeks later reached its subscriber in Virginia City, who promptly took it to the editorial office of the *Territorial Enterprise*, workplace not only of a young journalist named Mark Twain but also of William Wright, the editor responsible for the story.

*Mark Twain*

---

What is noteworthy about Jonathan Newhouse's home town is that William Wright, the author of the newspaper article, was also born and raised in Knox County, Ohio – a remarkable coincidence in view of the fact that Knox County, Ohio was a small town of 17,000 inhabitants. However, I am disposed to accept this in the same frame of mind usually assumed by Herodotus, the Father of History – that is to say, I am neither prepared to disbelieve it wholly nor to credit it without question. (For a biography of William Wright, alias Dan de Quille, see Richard A. Dwyer and Richard E. Lingenfelter: *Dan de Quille the Washoe Giant*, Reno 1990, p. 5 f.)

The latter picked up his pen and, his journalist's honour sorely wounded, supplied the additional information required by the haughty Briton.

'We are glad that the Telegraph has given us the opportunity, long awaited, of publishing in detail the sequel to the curious affair. [...] A fortnight after our account of the sad affair was published, we received a letter in regard to the matter from one David Baxter, who states that he is Justice of the Peace and ex-officio Coroner at Salt Wells [...] at the north end of Death Valley. "We find that the deceased [...] came to his death in Death Valley, Inyo County, California, on the 27th day of June, AD 1874, by being frozen in a sort of coat of sponge called a 'solar armor', of which he was the inventor and in which he was tightly laced at his own request, said 'solar armor' being moistened with some frigorific mixture, with the precise nature of which we are unacquainted."' However, there were clues as to the nature of the 'frigorific mixture' in a carpet bag which Mr Newhouse had left behind at the settlement. This contained bottles and jars of various sizes filled with all manner of fluids, powders and salts. One of the largest bottles was labelled 'Ether', another 'Bisulphide of Carbon', and others 'Ammonic Nitrate',

'Sodic Nitrate', 'Ammonic Chloride', 'Sodic Sulphate', and 'Sodic Phosphate'.

'Mr Baxter is firmly convinced,' William Wright went on, 'that with these chemicals, either alone or diluted with water, the degree of cold was produced which caused the death of the unfortunate man. He thinks that in his attempts to reach the fastenings of his armor, on his back, when he began to experience a painful degree of cold, he unavoidably compressed the india rubber pouch and thus constantly ejected more and more of the freezing cold fluid into the headpiece of his armor. As he stiffened in death, his arm, under which the sack was suspended, naturally pressed more strongly upon his side and thus caused a steady flow of the fluid. Mr Baxter is of the opinion that the frost and icicle found on the beard and depending from the nose of the deceased were formed from the water mingled with the more volatile fluids comprising the frigorific mixture.'

According to Mr Baxter, the men who discovered Mr Newhouse sustained appreciable frostbite in their hands when attempting to tie the corpse on a horse, because frigorific fluid oozed from the sponge whenever they touched it. They could not handle the corpse until they had cut it out of its armor. The latter was left behind in the desert.

'In conclusion, it only remains for us to state that Mr Baxter informed us that it was his intention to send the bottles and jars of chemicals to the Academy of Sciences at San Francisco; also the solar armor, in case he could recover it. Whether or not he has done so we cannot say. For several weeks we have closely watched the reports of the proceedings of the learned body named, but as yet have seen no mention of either the chemicals or the armor.'

It only remains for *us* to state that, at the time of writing, the Bulletin of the Academy of Sciences in San Francisco has never, at any time in the ensuing 180 years, reported receiving any of the chemicals referred to, let alone a sample of the solar armour.

# HAWIKU

One of the first Europeans to visit this part of the world was a Spaniard named Francisco Vásquez de Coronado. He had set off at the behest of the viceroy of Mexico City to discover the fabled 'Seven Cities of Cibola' in North America, which were rumoured to be an even more splendid sight than Tenochtitlan and Cuzco, with gates of turquoise, streets paved with silver, and cellars filled with gold and treasure. Accompanying him were 300 soldiers, twice as many Indian warriors, and three times as many draught horses to carry off the hoped-for booty, and his emergency supplies comprised 500 cattle and 5,000 sheep. Thirty years old, he doubtless cut an impressive figure in his gilded breastplate and plumed helmet. In case his favourite charger died, he had another 22 choice horses with him.

After four months, Coronado had crossed the Mojave Desert and, in an area known today as Arizona, come to a small town named Hawiku, which had been rumoured to be very large and wealthy. Coronado captured the place from its inhabitants, who were

*Francisco Vásquez de Coronado*

*Zuni Indian
pueblo*

armed with stones and arrows, and looted it thoroughly, only to discover that Hawiku was anything but a city of gold; it was a mud-brick *pueblo* inhabited by Zuni Indians. Slender-limbed and barely five feet tall, the Zuni were organized into a matrilineal, deeply religious community and maintained a peaceful culture of remarkable metaphysical refinement. They were also skilled basket-weavers and potters and knew how to coax abundant crops of maize, pumpkins and melons from the barren soil. In material terms, however, they led an extremely frugal existence in modest adobe huts that protected their almost naked bodies from the heat of summer and the cold of winter.

When their foreign visitor enquired after the Seven Golden Cities of Cibola, the Zuni shrugged their shoulders and, so as not to seem discourteous, pointed to the highlands in the west, where the magnificent and exceedingly wealthy city of Tusayan was said to be. On arriving there, however, all Coronado found was a terraced village inhabited by Hopi Indians and scarcely more comfortable than that of the Zuni.

The Hopi were another tribe who aspired to live in harmony with their natural surroundings and their fellow men. They prayed to the sun and were adept at dancing with snakes in their mouths, but they knew nothing of gold. Anxious to offer the strangers something, at least, they told Coronado of a mighty river, 20 days' march from their village, that flowed

*Hopi Indian performing a traditional snake dance*

towards the setting sun. This was of great interest to Coronado because a navigable river flowing into the Sea of Cortez would be excellently suited to opening up vast tracts of territory and, thus, worth plenty of gold from the colonial aspect.

Accordingly, Coronado sent his aide, García López de Cárdenas, to inspect this river with 25 soldiers and some Hopi guides. It must have been late in September 1540 and presumably not far from the spot where tourist helicopters from Las Vegas land today that Cárdenas became the first white man to stand on the

*Grand Canyon*

southern lip of the Grand Canyon, where the world suddenly ended and the maws of hell seemed to yawn. He correctly estimated the distance across at three to four miles, but he was disappointed by the river the Hopi had guided him to.

'Is that supposed to be a mighty river?' Cárdenas demanded, having recovered from his initial shock and glimpsed a thread of silver far below. 'It's a little stream no more than six feet wide. No ship could navigate it.'

'The river is very wide indeed, at least half a mile,' the Hopi assured him. 'It looks much narrower only because it's so far down and we're so high up.'

'No canyon can be so deep that it makes a wide river look like a narrow stream,' Cárdenas retorted, but in order to provide his superior officer, Coronado, with reliable information he instructed three of his soldiers to descend the rocky side of the Grand Canyon and inspect the river at close quarters.

His scouts spent three days combing the edge of the

canyon for a way down. At last, early on the morning of the fourth, they ventured over the side. At four that afternoon they returned.

'How far down did you go?' asked Cárdenas.

'About a third of the way,' the scouts told him.

'Well?'

'The Indians are right. The river is at least half a mile wide.'

'I don't believe it.'

'You see those boulders down there on the river bank? How big do you think they are?'

'I don't know. The height of a man, let's say.'

'Wrong,' said the scouts. 'They're bigger than the Golden Tower in Seville. What's more, the river is full of rapids. Navigating it is out of the question.'

*Hopi Indian*

Cárdenas now proposed to ride downstream and see if the foaming torrent became calmer and more navigable further west, but the Hopi were averse to this. They knew, of course, that the lower reaches of the Colorado River were calmer, and that it flowed westwards, wide and easily navigable, to the Gulf of California. They also knew that there was an easy route to its lower reaches through pleasantly shady, wooded countryside. However, the Hopi had no desire to show the Spaniards this route because it led through their tribal territory, and they guessed that no good would come of those pale-faced strangers with their gleaming armour and terrifying firearms. So they strongly advised Cárdenas not to undertake a pointless ride to the west, where all that awaited him was not gold but hunger, thirst and an agonizing death in a fearsome desert. In his place, they said, they would ride east.

By the time Cárdenas returned and reported to General Coronado, the latter had already decided to ride east. A runaway slave, whom Coronado had christened 'the Turk' because of his physiognomy, had told him of his native city, Quivira, which abounded in gold and silver and was traversed by a river several miles wide in which the fish grew as big as cows, and which the people of Quivira navigated in 20-man canoes whose prows were adorned with eagle statuettes of solid gold. So Coronado and his army followed the Turk to New Mexico, looting, murdering and raping as they went. They spent a whole year astray in the endless prairies of Texas, Oklahoma and Kansas, where millions of buffalo grazed, but they never found any appreciable quantity of gold. In the summer of 1541, Coronado was compelled to acknowledge that Quivira was just a wretched village, composed of thatched hovels on the banks of the Kansas River, whose inhabitants

*Buffalo*

went around almost naked and ate their buffalo meat raw. The Turk had invented the myth of gold and silver in order to persuade the Spaniards to escort him safely home past all the hostile tribes en route. Coronado had him garrotted for his pains, and then, homesick for his wife, rode back to Mexico City, where he arrived in autumn 1542 with only a hundred soldiers, exhausted, saddened, and deeply ashamed of his gullibility.

Meanwhile the Hopi, whose white lie had gained them another 250 years' freedom from disturbance by Spanish invaders, resumed their peaceful, *pueblo* way of life.

# FLAGSTAFF

My journey from the Grand Canyon back to Olten took me in almost exactly the direction Coronado might have taken if he hadn't fallen for the lies of the Hopi and the Turk. I spent my last night in Flagstaff, Arizona. When I drove out of the town the next morning, I found myself back on the celebrated Route 66.

It was a profoundly depressing experience.

I saw scores of motorcyclists pursuing their dreams of another existence on that highway, riding along it for hour after hour at a steady 80 m.p.h. On the occasions when they did alight from the saddle, they strode around stiff-legged amid the sun-bleached Coca-Cola cans and tyre-flattened rabbits on the hard shoulder, relieved themselves against Joshua trees, and stared blankly out across the Mojave Desert. And because no trace of their dream could be seen there, they folded up their stands again and rode on in pursuit of it, eyes glued to the point at which the road disappeared over the horizon.

One could tell from their apprehensively hunched shoulders that they were no Easy Riders in real life, but architects, accountants or plumbers from London, Düsseldorf or Barcelona.

They had shelled out a lot of money and spun their alimony-entitled ex-wives a yarn in order to fly here just once in their lives and rent these Harleys on deposit from an outfitter who had also sold them brand-new fringed leather jackets, steel-tipped boots and black helmets adorned with 'Street Devils', or something of the kind, in white runic script.

And now they were riding in gaggles, hour after hour, along this highway where the gas stations sell their wares at twice or three times the usual price because it's only here that tourists are dumb enough to embark on a ride across the desert with half-empty tanks. Their backsides ached and their hands were benumbed by the vibrations of the technologically obsolete Harley engines, and the tour operator's escorting truck followed on behind with their trolley bags, so they could put on their McGregor shirts and ironed jeans for supper at the Holiday Inn. And they had their toothbrushes and blood-pressure pills with them, and each of them had a Rolex on his wrist and an iPhone in the breast pocket of his fringed jacket. Many of them had turned off their mobile phones, but they'd taken them along for safety's sake, and were careful to ensure that they were kept fully charged.

*Riding along Route 66*

Every 20 seconds they peered through their mirrored Ray Bans at the speedometer and estimated from their mileage and average speed how long it would be before they reached their next scheduled stop and could fold down their stands once more.

I don't know if these Easy Riders are aware of it, but Route 66 is an old camel track. After the Mexican-American War of 1846–8 the youthful United States acquired 529,000 square miles of arid, dusty desert in Arizona, New Mexico, Nevada, Colorado, Utah and California – terrain as alien to most Americans as Ukraine or Mongolia.

This *terra incognita* had to be crossed by pioneers on their way to the promised land of California, where nuggets of gold were reputed to spill from every furrow and orange trees bore fruit three times a year. The only problem was that it was impassable, as far as one could tell, because there were no roads, no navigable rivers, and no waterholes – not even any discernible tracks. Horses died of thirst, mules collapsed from exhaustion, draught oxen dropped dead, and humans got hopelessly lost and also expired after slaughtering the last of their beasts. Then there were the Indians who mysteriously managed to move around with ease in this hostile environment and stubbornly resisted the pale-faced intruders. It wasn't to be expected that they would be willing to act as guides for Washington.

So the Americans recalled who had guided their European forebears across the deserts of the Old World: the nomads of Arabia on their camels. The US Army decided to acquire some Arabian camels to show them the way to the West.

On 2 March 1855 the United States Congress approved a credit of $30,000 to enable camels to be introduced into the heart of the North American continent, where there were neither navigable rivers nor passable roads. The purpose of the operation was to keep the nomadic Indian tribes who were constantly 'rebelling against civilization' in check, and to open up trade routes and facilitate communication.

Since the camels were to be under military command, a naval transport vessel was acquired and equipped with spacious stables on the upper deck. On the morning of 3 June 1855 the USS *Supply* sailed from New York for North Africa, and on 4 August she dropped anchor in the picturesque little harbour of Tunis. The two officers in command, Major Henry C. Wayne and Lieutenant David Dixon Porter, undertook their first trip ashore. In all their American innocence, they informed the cattle dealers of the harbour district that they were Americans, had many thousands of dollars to spend, and were firmly determined to purchase a camel – possibly more than one. They then bought the first camel they were offered by the first dealer they came to for the first price he quoted.

Wayne and Porter were hardly back on board the USS *Supply* when they discovered that the animal was suffering from camelpox, a disease so infectious, unpleasant and difficult to treat that the Arabs proverbially wished it upon their enemies. The two Americans could not but regard it as an insult when, on

*The USS* Supply

the following day, the governor of Tunis sent them two more camels in little better condition. To spare themselves further humiliation, Wayne and Porter sailed on, intending to do business more shrewdly in Turkey, Persia or Egypt.

But healthy camels were hard to find anywhere in the Mediterranean area because most of them were being used as pack animals in the Crimean War on the Russo-Turkish border. Major Wayne and Lieutenant Porter sailed to Malta, Greece and Turkey, where, although they purchased no camels, they were able to learn something about the camel trade. They learnt that two-humped Asiatic camels were best suited to carrying loads, whereas single-humped Arab dromedaries were used mainly for riding. They learnt to tell healthy camels from sick and discovered that many camel dealers injected the limp humps of sick beasts with water to make them appear healthier. They also learnt that a healthy camel cow could be bought for between 40 and 50 dollars, and a good bull for 75 to 100, and that the Tunisian dealer responsible for their first purchase had brazenly swindled them. They sold two of their three sick camels to a Constantinople butcher for 44 dollars.

They eventually found an abundant supply of healthy, inexpensive animals in the camel markets of Egypt, because the viceroy, Mohammed Ali Pasha, had prohibited the exportation of camels

*Embarking camels on the USS* Supply

by decree. After lengthy negotiations they finally managed to acquire 33 camels and five Ottoman camel drivers in Alexandria and Smyrna and get them aboard their ship.

The USS *Supply* set sail for Texas on 15 February 1856. The two-month return trip across the wintry Atlantic was stormy, and the camels had to be lashed to the deck in a kneeling position. It is apparent from the captain's log that the animals were not actually seasick, but that severe storms robbed them of their appetite for hay. When the ship entered Indianola harbour, Texas, on

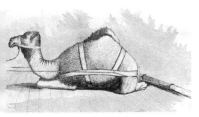

*Camel lashed down aboard the USS* Supply *during a storm*

73

29 April 1856, there were 34 animals on board – one more than there had been when she sailed.

In June 1857 the caravan set off from Albuquerque to find a westward route across the desert along the 35th parallel. It comprised 44 men, 12 covered wagons, 25 camels, and numerous horses, mules and dogs.

For the first few days the camels tried the soldiers' patience by lagging far behind the horses and mules, but they demonstrated their superiority as soon as water ran short. Unerringly, they led the caravan many miles to the next waterhole – of whose existence neither soldiers nor horses had known – and then watched dispassionately as men and beasts greedily jostled for a drink.

After that the camels and their Ottoman drivers assumed the caravan's undisputed leadership, unfailingly guiding it along the shortest, quickest and safest route to California past canyons, craters, volcanoes and the remains of Indian civilizations that had failed to survive a visit from the Conquistadors. It was a 'constant source of wonder' to the leader of the expedition, Edward Fitzgerald Beale, and his companions, that they could scarcely cover a mile of their journey without coming across ruins or fragments of pottery that bore witness to the erstwhile presence in large numbers of 'a race whose very name has passed away', as Beale noted in his journal.

*Camel caravan in California*

Late in August they came to the big pueblo of the Zuni Indians, whose 12,000 inhabitants still lived as they had done in the days of the Spanish explorer Francisco Coronado. Finally, on 17 October, after a four-month trek covering 1,200 miles, the camel caravan reached the Colorado River and halted at a place now called Beale's Crossing, 15 miles north of the small Californian town of Needles. There they were closely watched by the Mohave Indians, who had already had some contact with passing gold prospectors and expressed their surprise at the camels' appearance in fractured English. 'God damn my soul eyes!' one of them exclaimed, according to expedition leader Beale. 'How de do! How de do!'

From that summer onwards, settlers undertaking the great trek to California in their covered wagons followed the tracks of those 25 camels through the Mojave Desert. The dangerous routes through Death Valley

*Asiatic camel in British Columbia, Canada, in May 1862*

and across the snow-covered passes of the Sierra Nevada were no longer used.

The 25 camels remained in California. The army sold them in November 1863 to zoos, travelling circuses and mining companies. The animals left behind in Texas were released and the Ottoman camel drivers returned to Egypt – all save one, who remained in America, got married, and became a scout for the US Army. Jordanian by birth, his name was Hadji Ali, but because his comrades couldn't remember such an outlandish appellation they christened him 'Hi Jolly'. When the army no longer required his services, Hi Jolly bought a mule and rode off into Arizona's Sonoran Desert to dig for copper, gold and silver in the Plomosa and Harquahala Mountains. He died in Quartzsite, Arizona, on 16 December 1903, at the age of 75.

Some time after Hi Jolly's death an old prospector swore to a strange story that definitely has the unmistakable ring of truth, even though it may not have happened exactly the way he told it. According to him, he had spotted an old red camel in the desert near Quartzsite and had mentioned this incredible encounter in a saloon. A dark-skinned, elderly man had thereupon asked him where he had seen the camel and, on being told, had left the saloon without another word. The dark-skinned old man – according to legend, none other than Hi Jolly – had been found dead in the desert a few days later, with his arms around the neck of the red camel, which had also expired.

*Wedding photograph of Hadji Ali and his bride*

Hi Jolly's tomb is situated a few hundred feet from US Highway 60 and takes the form of a pyramid with a camel perched on its apex. His remains are buried inside it, together with the ashes of a camel that died in Los Angeles Zoo in 1934.

When the Santa Fe Railroad from Los Angeles to Kansas was built from 1869 onwards, the track precisely followed in the camels' footsteps and retraced

*Hadji Ali
(Hi Jolly)*

the covered wagons' route through the Mojave Desert. And half a century later, when automobiles were invented and US Highway 66 became the first through road from east to west, its engineers took their bearings from the railroad, in other words, from the covered wagons' route and, ultimately, from the trail blazed by Ottoman scouts on their camels.

The last descendant of Hadji Ali's camels is reported to have been sighted in British Columbia in the mid 1930s, but many sources claim it was a Chinese camel. That, however, is another story.

*Hi Jolly's tomb in Quartzsite, Arizona*

# Illustrations

p. 12 – *Wells Fargo wagon*. John C. H. Grabill Collection, Library of Congress 1890.

p. 15 – *Senator William W. Stewart*. Courtesy of Roy Jones.

p. 18 – *Josef Munzinger. Die Schweizer Bundesräte*, a biographical dictionary, p. 121.

p. 22 – *Adolf Hitler*. Heinrich Hoffmann photo, 1936.

p. 23 – *Ernst Gustav Munzinger*. ZVG.

p. 26 – *The big ore-crushing mill, Panamint City*. L. Burr Belden, U.S. Borax Company.

p. 27 – *Panamint City today*. Photo by Gabriel Moulin.

p. 33 – *Typical saloon tent in Death Valley*. The Huntington Library, San Marino, California 1895.

p. 34 – *Hotel*. Marcia Rittenhaus Wynn: *Desert Bonanza: The Story of Early Randsburg, Mojave Desert Mining Camp*, M. W. Samuelson, Culver City 1949.

p. 36 – *Mine shaft entrance, Skidoo*. Craig MacDonald: *Ghost Town Glimpses*, Antheion Press Inc., San Francisco 1975.

p. 40 – *Joe 'Hootch' Simpson hanged for the second time*. Eastern California Museum, Independence, California.

p. 42 – Newspaper cutting, 3 June 1908, © *The New York Times*.

p. 43 – *Dr Reginald MacDonald with an unknown patient.* Marcia Rittenhaus Wynn: *Desert Bonanza: The Story of Early Randsburg, Mojave Desert Mining Camp*, M. W. Samuelson, Culver City 1949.

p. 49 – Newspaper cutting, 10 July 1874, © *The New York Times*.

p. 50 – *William Wright, alias Dan de Quille.* Special Collections, Getchell Library, University of Nevada, Reno.

p. 51 – *Mark Twain.* Library of Congress 1867.

p. 57 – *Francisco Vásquez de Coronado.* Frederic Remington Art Museum.

p. 58 – *Zuni Indian pueblo.* J. K. Hillers, U.S. Geographical Survey.

p. 59 – *Hopi Indian performing a traditional snake dance.* Native Americans 1946.

p. 63 – *Buffalo.* © Jack Dyckinga.

p. 69 – *Riding along Route 66.* © 'Caveman Chuck' Coker.

p. 71 – *The USS* Supply. Library of Congress.

p. 73 – *Embarking camels on the USS* Supply. From Jefferson Davis's report to the Secretary of War, 1856.

p. 75 – *Camel caravan*. U.S. Bureau of Public Roads, National Archives.

p. 76 – *Asiatic camel in British Columbia in May 1862.* © Royal B.C. Museum.

p. 77 – *Wedding photograph of Hadji Ali and his bride.* Arizona Historical Society.

p. 79 – *Hi Jolly's tomb in Quartzsite, Arizona.* Chris Emmett, *Texas Camel Tales*, Steck-Vaughn Company. Austin 1932.